Special Days, Special Dances

Tracy Tse

A Harcourt Achieve Imprint

www.Rigby.com
1-800-531-5015

Hi! I'm Tracy. I love to dance!
I go to a class where I learn
Chinese dances.
Most of the dances I've done
are for special days.

My favorite special day is the
Chinese New Year.
It starts in January or February,
and it lasts for fifteen days!
We eat special food and visit friends.

The last day of the Chinese New Year is the Lantern Festival.
All of the colored lights are beautiful!

One of the best things about the
Chinese New Year is the Lion Dance.
The dancers make the lions run
through the crowd.

I wanted to find out more about the dances people do on special days.

I asked my teacher, Ms. Ortiz,
and my friend, Greg,
to help me.

Tracy: Mrs. Ortiz, can you tell me about Cinco de Mayo?

Mrs. Ortiz: Cinco De Mayo happens on May 5.
It is a special day for Mexicans and Mexican Americans.

People have big parties with their families and friends.

Mrs. Ortiz: My children Marta and Lupe dance with their friends every Cinco de Mayo.
The girls twist and twirl.

Their dresses have very full skirts.
They wear pretty ribbons in their hair.

Tracy: Greg, what do you and your family do during Kwanzaa?

Greg: My family has a big party in December for Kwanzaa. We tell stories and open gifts. We also light red, green, and black candles.

13

Greg: The last night of Kwanzaa is December 31.
This night is called *Karamu*.
Last year we ate a big dinner.
I sang songs with my brother and sister.

We also watched African dancers.
They danced to the drum music.
They moved their feet so fast!

I've learned so much
from my friends.
Maybe I can teach them
some of my favorite dances!